W9-BUR-233

A

COOKBOOK

FOR

MILLENNIALS

AND LITERALLY ANYONE ELSE BUT IDK IF THE JOKES WILL MAKE SENSE SORRY :(

BY CALEB COUTURIE ILLUSTRATOR BENJ ZELLER

CAMERON + COMPANY

This book is dedicated to my original personal chefs: my parents.
Thanks for turning off the Xbox and dragging me into the kitchen.

I'm sorry I was such a shit.
And kinda still am.

Love you. <3

TABLE OF CONTENTS

BREAKFAST · 6

LUNCH · 22

APPS & SIDES · 32

DINNER · 40

DESSERT · 54

I AM NOT A CHEF.

In fact, I'm twenty-three years old, which means I'm nothing but stressed, confused, and hungry. I was born in 1996, on the cusp of two generations: Gen Z and, of course, millennials.

We're the avocado-toast-eating, labradoodle-toting, sensitive, succulent-loving radicals of the world. We complain about the cost of education and health care, but we also buy $300 antique record players. What can I say? We're not perfect.

And as a millennial, one thing I've learned about my fellow millennials is that we're pretty busy. Between paying off thousands in loans, working sixty-hour shifts at unpaid internships, and dealing with the constant dread of being handed a planet in a political-economic-social-climate shitstorm . . . well, you get the point.

Most of us don't have the time, let alone desire, to learn to cook.

LIKE I SAID, I'M NOT A CHEF.

But I am a millennial. And I can cook pretty fucking decently.

More important, I can cook realistically.

On a budget. Strapped for time. Having a mental breakdown.

In other words, I know recipes millennials can actually make.

These are the recipes for when you're just too fucking high, but you also just neeeeed food. Or a celebratory meal for when your parents Venmo you grocery money.

So, let's get cooking. But not right now.

Finish whichever episode of *The Office* you're watching first.

BREAK FAST

BREAKFAST IS THE BEST MEAL.
IT'S JUST AN OBJECTIVE FACT.

BREAKFAST GIVES YOU THE FREEDOM TO EAT 2,500
CALORIES WHEN YOU WAKE UP, THEN FALL ASLEEP
UNTIL IT'S DARK OUT.

YOU CAN EAT CAKE, LITERAL CAKE, AT 9 A.M. AND NO ONE
WILL BAT AN EYE (AS LONG AS YOUR CAKE IS IN PAN FORM).

OH, AND DID I MENTION BACON? YEAH. BACON.

IF I'M BEING HONEST, I LOVE BREAKFAST MORE THAN I LOVE
MOST HUMAN BEINGS. EXCEPT MERYL STREEP.
SHE IS A NATIONAL TREASURE, AND WE MUST PROTECT HER.

CEREAL

Please tell me you don't actually need directions for how to make cereal.

WHAT YOU NEED:

A box of cereal. Nothing with "cookies" in the name, or anything that spells "fruit" with two "O's."

Milk. Any kind really. Whole, 1%, 2%, skim, goat, oat, soy, almond. It's 2021, I'm pretty sure you can milk rocks at this point.

WHAT YOU DO:

1 Pour cereal into a bowl. Or mug. Or plastic container. Pretty much anything except a plate.

2 Pour milk over the cereal until you can just barely see the milk through the cereal itself. Anddd boom. Done.

3 Reconsider your life choices because you're reading about how to make cereal.

SCRAMBLED EGGS

Alright, we're actually using a stove top now.
Don't let the success go to your head.

WHAT YOU NEED:

2 eggs (no shit)

Splash of milk

Pinch of pepper

Pinch of salt

Optional: pinch of garlic
   and onion powder

WHAT YOU DO:

1   Place a pan over medium heat and let that warm up for about 2 to 3 minutes.

2   Crack the eggs into a bowl. Add in a small splash of milk, as well as your seasonings, then stir until everything is incorporated.

3   Lightly butter or spray your warm pan, then pour in your egg mixture.

4   Cook for about 90 seconds, or until the eggs are cooked to about 90 percent of the consistency you like. Turn off the burner and remove the pan from heat. The eggs will continue to cook that final 10 percent once you've turned off the heat.

5   Idk that's it.

FRIED EGGS (OVER EASY)

Because eventually you're going to get tired of scrambled eggs.

WHAT YOU NEED:

The same exact shit as the scrambled eggs recipe, except no milk.

WHAT YOU DO:

1 Place a pan over medium heat and let it warm up for 2 to 3 minutes. Lightly butter/oil your pan.

2 Crack your eggs directly into the pan. No bowl this time, which means fewer dishes, which means more time avoiding your other responsibilities.

3 While the eggs begin to cook, sprinkle your seasonings directly on top of the eggs.

4 For over-easy eggs, allow your eggs to cook for about 90 seconds, or until the eggs are just sturdy enough for you to flip. For over medium, cook for 2 minutes, or until you see a white layer start to develop over the eggs. For over hard, cook until the yolk has gone from a rich, runny yellow, to a pale, stiffer texture.

5 Once you reach the overness you're happy with, flip 'em. Cook for another 10 seconds, then remove from heat.

6 EMERGENCY BROKEN-YOLK STEP: Don't worry, if you break a yolk, just blame boomers.

BACON

The breakfast meat your girlfriend told you not to worry about.

WHAT YOU NEED:

Good, thick-cut bacon. You can cut corners on a lot of things in life, but bacon is not one of them. Save the money you would've spent on another tattoo and invest in some goddamn bacon.

WHAT YOU DO:

1 Preheat your oven, YES YOUR OVEN, to 400 degrees.

2 Line a baking sheet with aluminum foil, then spread bacon onto the sheet spaced just far enough so that each piece isn't touching.

3 Bake for 20 to 25 minutes, or until the bacon has reached a crispness of your liking.

4 If you, like I, grew up with bacon made in a pan, take a bite of the bacon you just made. Now, call your parents and yell at them for subjecting you to a life of insufficient pork products.

MAPLE BACON

It's like normal bacon but 200 percent better and 300 percent less healthy. It's fucking rad.

WHAT YOU NEED:

Good bacon. We've been over this.

¼ cup maple syrup

¼ cup brown sugar

WHAT YOU DO:

1 Do the same exact thing you did for the normal bacon, but once you've lined your baking sheet with bacon, spread the maple syrup and brown sugar evenly over each strip. Use a spoon to make sure all the bacon is covered evenly.

2 After baking that shit for 25 minutes, give your mouth the gift of what's basically just edible cocaine.

BREAKFAST BURRITO

The perfect on-the-go snack to take while you cry in the car on your way to work.

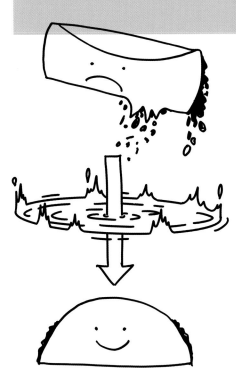

WHAT YOU DO:

1 Preheat a pan over medium heat and make the scrambled eggs I taught you about earlier. Then leave those to cool off on the side.

2 Make some form of meat. If it's oven bacon, great. If it's not, that's cool too. Just cook it until it's brown and let it cool. Pretty much the golden rule of cooking meat.

3 Keep a pan hot! Once you've got your eggs and breakfast meat ready, lay a tortilla out onto a plate, then immediately add your meat, eggs, cheese, and other stuff into the burrito. To roll your burrito, either close your eyes and wish really hard, or look up a video on YouTube.

4 Place the burrito back into your hot pan to grill both sides so that they're nice and crispy.

5 Alternate universe: Fail to roll the burrito correctly and enjoy a delicious oversize taco.

BREAKFAST HASH

BECAUSE NOTHING SAYS "I WANT TO HAVE A PRODUCTIVE START TO MY DAY" LIKE EATING A PACKAGE OF FRIED POTATOES.

ME AFTER EATING THIS

WHAT YOU NEED:

Canola oil

½ pound ground pork or turkey sausage

Chopped veggies of choice, but onions and bell peppers recommended

1 package frozen hash browns. No one has time to peel and shred their own potatoes, Karen.

3 eggs

½ cup cheddar cheese

Egg seasonings

WHAT YOU DO:

1 Preheat your oven to 375 degrees.

2 Place two pans over medium-high heat and allow those to warm up. In one of the two pans, coat the bottom with a thin layer of canola oil, about ¼ cup, but I won't tell if you use more.

3 Once the pans are heated, in the pan without oil, place your ground sausage and veggies. Let those cook until the meat is nice and browned all the way through and the veggies have sweat and developed some color. In the pan with the preheated oil, fry enough hash browns to put you in a moderate, but not excessive, food coma.

4 Once your hash browns are golden and your meat and veggies are cooked, combine the two in one oven-safe pan. Most pans are oven-safe, and even if you fuck yours up, you bought it for $10 as part of a set from Costco. Calm down. Anywayyy, make three egg-sized divots in your potato/meat/veggie mixture, then crack the eggs directly inside those divots. Lastly, spread the cheese over the entire pan and season to taste, then let the whole thing bake in your preheated oven for 10 to 12 minutes.

5 After allowing 5 minutes to cool, enjoy. Remember, I'm not responsible for the noises your body will make after your first bite.

PANCAKES

Just buy pancake mix. Not gonna bother with this.

NEXT

CRUNCHY FRENCH TOAST

You know all those times when you ate French toast and thought, *Wow, this could use more carbs*. You're in luck.

WHAT YOU NEED:

Milk, about ½ cup

3 eggs

Pinch of cinnamon

Splash of vanilla extract

Bread. Anything but whole wheat. That's just salad.

3 cups cornflakes

WHAT YOU DO:

1 Preheat your oven to 375 degrees *and* a pan over medium heat.

2 In a bowl wide enough to dip a piece of bread in (foreshadowing), combine your milk, eggs, cinnamon, and vanilla. Also, take your cornflakes and crush them up in a plastic bag. Save those for later.

3 Briefly, and I mean like maybe 3 seconds on each side, dip your slices of bread into your French toast batter. While still wet, coat each side of the bread in your crushed cornflakes.

4 Thoroughly butter your preheated pan, then panfry each piece of French toast for about 2 to 3 minutes on each side, or until the outside of the bread and cornflakes have developed some golden brown color.

5 After panfrying, place your crunchy French toast onto a baking sheet and bake them for about 8 to 10 minutes.

6 Take a bite. If you're not religious, grapple with what you just went through. You may have just met God.

CINNAMON ROLL FRENCH TOAST

IF YOU LIKE SUGAR AND NAPPING AT 11 A.M., THIS IS THE ONE FOR YOU.

100%
HEART
ATTACK
JUICE

WHAT YOU NEED:

¼ cup butter

1 package cinnamon roll
   dough (comes w/ icing)

The ingredients for
   French toast batter from
   the previous recipe.
   Sorry, I'm lazy.

½ cup maple syrup

WHAT YOU DO:

1 Preheat your oven to 375 degrees.

2 Melt your butter in the microwave for about 25 seconds. Use half of the melted butter to coat the bottom of an oven-safe pan, then save the other half to add to your French toast batter.

3 Open your cinnamon roll dough and break the dough into small, bite-size pieces. Aim for like 50 total, but honestly, it doesn't fucking matter. Do you. Spread those evenly across your pan.

4 Make your French toast batter, adding in the remaining melted butter. Pour the batter directly over the pieces of dough, and then pour the maple syrup over that. Put your pan of sugary dough balls directly into the oven and let it bake for about 25 minutes.

5 Remove your pan from the oven and allow to cool. After about 3 minutes of cooling, add your icing.

6 After eating, contact your doctor. Run a few tests. Just make sure everything's working right in the ol' arteries.

THE DUTCH BABY

It's a pancake that's inflated.
I'm sure you, as a millennial, know nothing about inflation.

WHAT YOU NEED:

6 eggs. Invest in a
  chicken if you plan
  on making this often.

1½ cups milk

1½ cups flour

¾ cup of butter. It's gonna
  look like a lot, but that's
  only because it is a lot.

WHAT YOU DO:

1 Preheat your oven to 425 degrees. PUT YOUR (ideally, cast iron) PAN IN THE OVEN WHILE IT PREHEATS. I can't stress how important that is. Hopefully, the CAPS will do it.

2 In a blender, mix your eggs, milk, and flour until they create a smooth mixture with no lumps. Pro tip: put the flour in the blender last.

3 Once your oven reaches about 375, put the butter in your pre-heating pan and allow that to melt inside the oven. By the time the oven hits 425, the butter should be completely melted.

4 When the oven hits 425, pour your batter directly into the butter-soaked pan and let that bake for 25 to 30 minutes. I recommend closer to 30 for the best form, color, and texture.

5 Take a picture of the most beautiful thing you've ever made in the kitchen. Actually, what am I saying? This is the most beautiful thing you've ever made. Anywhere. The good news is that it will be delicious. The bad news is that it's all downhill from here. Speaking of . . .

U.S. MINIMUM WAGE INFLATION
REPRESENTED IN SERVINGS OF PANCAKES

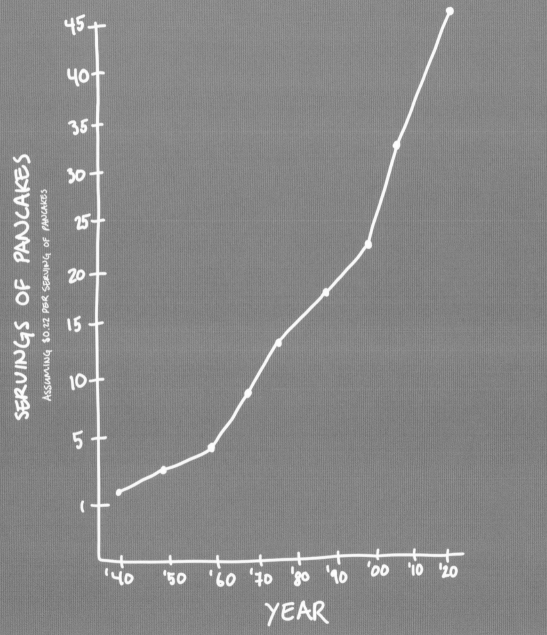

SERVINGS OF PANCAKES

ASSUMING $0.22 PER SERVING OF PANCAKES

YEAR

SOURCE: HUFFPOST

21

LUNCH

IN MY OPINION, LUNCH DREW THE SHORT STICK.
SANDWICHED (LOL) BETWEEN THE HOLIEST OF MEALS
(BREAKFAST) AND THE HEARTIEST OF MEALS (DINNER),
LUNCH TENDS TO GET OVERLOOKED.

BUT LOOK, LUNCH IS MORE THAN JUST A WEIRD-SOUNDING
WORD. IT'S A DOWNRIGHT OKAY PART OF THE DAY.
SURE, LUNCH MAY BE THE MEAL YOU EAT IN THE BATHROOM
STALL AT WORK, BUT WHY NOT MAKE THAT MEAL GREAT?

LET'S GIVE LUNCH THE CHANCE IT DESERVES.
I PROMISE THESE NEXT FEW RECIPES WILL BE BETTER
THAN THE LEFTOVER PIZZA SITTING IN YOUR FRIDGE. . . .
THEN AGAIN, THERE'S A SALAD IN THIS SECTION.

HONESTLY, THE PIZZA MIGHT BE BETTER.

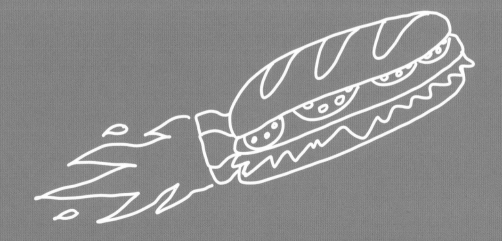

CAESAR SALAD AND DRESSING

The perfect meal to make on a Monday after a long weekend of drinking, doing drugs, and eating garbage.

WHAT YOU NEED:

A box of green leafed products of your choosing. I use arugula, but I recognize romaine as the overwhelming favorite. If you wanna go crazy, use kale.

¼ cup of olive oil

¼ cup of lemon juice

2 teaspoons Dijon mustard

Salt and pepper, to taste

WHAT YOU DO:

1 Wash your greens. If they came prewashed, wash them anyway (and dry them so your salad isn't gross and wet), then put them in a bowl.

2 Mix every ingredient except the lettuce in a bowl. The resulting liquidy stuff is your dressing. Now, pour that over your salad and give it a toss.

3 Post a picture to social media so people can see how health-conscious you are. And don't forget to eat two desserts tonight for being so good.

SLOW COOKER BBQ CHICKEN

If you don't have a slow cooker, get one. They're like $15 *and* get this:
They do all the cooking for you (slowly).

WHAT YOU NEED:

3 pounds boneless skin-less chicken breast

1½ cups BBQ sauce of your choice

¼ cup brown sugar

Salt, pepper, garlic, and onion powder, to taste

WHAT YOU DO:

1 Put all the ingredients in your slow cooker, and give it a good mix to make sure everything is evenly incorporated over your chicken. Brown goo is the general consistency you're looking for.

2 Turn slow cooker on low for 6 to 8 hours or high for 3 to 4.

3 Leave for a bit. Go on a walk. Meet someone. Fall in love. Get married. Buy a house. Have kids. (Or don't.) Grow old together. But don't forget that in 3 to 8 hours your chicken will be done.

4 Take two forks and, inside your slow cooker, shred the chicken. And just like that, you're all done. Now you have chicken and a mortgage. Look at you.

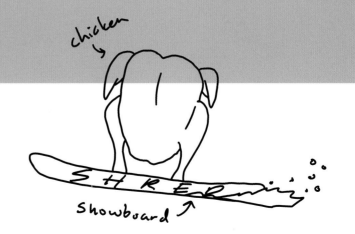

chicken

SHREDDING

Showboard

SOUP

UNPOPULAR OPINION BUT:

fuck soup.

BEST DELI SANDWICH EVER

It'll be just like that sandwich chain, but without the creepy spokesperson who touches kids.

WHAT YOU NEED:

Pick up to 3: Turkey, chicken, steak, ham, pastrami, corned beef, roast beef. The list goes on. Anything other than tuna.

Bread roll. Or slices. I don't care.

Cheese slices of your choosing

Fixings. Just pick some. I'm clearly not one to tell you how to live your life. Unless you put pineapple on pizza. Then I'm calling the cops.

WHAT YOU DO:

1 Line a baking sheet with foil, and preheat your oven to 350 degrees.

2 Add your meat to your sliced bread, then top with a slice of cheese of your choosing. With the sandwich spread out open-faced, bake your sandwich in the oven at 350 for 10 minutes, or simply stick it in a toaster oven set to "toast" for 5 minutes.

3 Remove, and while still warm, add the fixings of your choosing. Whatever you do, you can't go wrong by adding a little chipotle mayo to any sandwich.

4 Now that you're well-versed in rocket science, apply to NASA.

GRILLED CHEESE

The thing you eat when you're sick. Or when you're feeling nostalgic. Or on a Tuesday at 10:23 P.M.

WHAT YOU NEED:

¼ cup of butter

Bread. 2 slices. Sourdough. Don't play games.

A good handful of cheese. Sliced or shredded. Cheddar preferred.

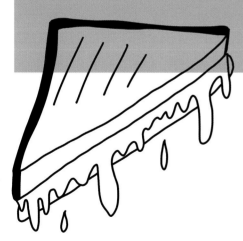

WHAT YOU DO:

1 Preheat a pan over medium heat.

2 When your pan is hot, generously butter the pan using half of your butter. Place a slice of bread directly onto the hot butter, then stack your cheese on top. Lastly, add your top slice of bread. Allow that to cook for 2 to 3 minutes on one side.

3 Using a spatula, lift your sandwich up and once again butter your pan using the other half. Then, flip the sandwich and cook the other side.

4 Optional: If you're feeling fancy as fuck, add a layer of cheese directly onto the pan and place your sandwich on top. Let that cook for about 30 seconds and you'll have a fried cheese-crusted grilled cheese. The thought alone brings tears to my eyes.

MEATBALL SANDWICH

NOW HERE'S SOMETHING I CAN GET BEHIND. IT'S BASICALLY PIZZA AS A SANDWICH. THAT'S THE KIND OF INGENUITY I HOPE AI IS BRINGING INTO THE 2020s.

WHAT YOU NEED:

1 pound ground pork

1 egg

¼ cup bread crumbs

¼ cup Parmesan cheese,
  plus more for garnish

¼ cup parsley

Salt and pepper, to taste

Garlic and onion powder,
  to taste (optional)

Roll, technically of your choosing, but choose Dutch Crunch

¼ cup shredded
  mozzarella cheese

1 jar marinara sauce

SAD

WHAT YOU DO:

1 Preheat a pan over medium-high heat.

2 Mix your ground pork, egg, bread crumbs, Parmesan, parsley, salt, and pepper together. Add some garlic and onion powder if you're feeling dangerous. Now roll that mixture into ideal eating size (to each their own), but I recommend keeping them on the smaller size so they cook faster.

3 Fry your meatballs in the pan with just a tiny splash of oil, making sure to cook all sides evenly until they've developed a dark brown crust.

4 While the meatballs cook, remember the good times. Before the break up. The road trips. The late-night pizza runs. Your one special spot on the pier. Oh, young love. If only you could go back . . . While you're spiraling, slice your roll and layer each side with mozzarella cheese. Toast in a toaster oven, or broil on low for about 2 to 3 minutes, checking to make sure it doesn't burn.

5 Right before your meatballs finish cooking, turn off the heat and add some marinara sauce to the pan. Move it around until the sauce completely coats your meatballs.

6 Put your meatballs and sauce onto your perfectly toasted roll, sprinkle with some Parmesan, and enjoy. Or don't, because now you're thinking about the one who got away.

APPS & SIDES

APPETIZERS ARE HONESTLY JUST FUCKING GREAT.

APPS CAN BE CHEESY, GREASY, FRIED, OR FLUFFY.

THEY'RE ALMOST ALWAYS A GREAT DEAL.

BUT MOST IMPORTANTLY, LIKE EVERYTHING IN THE LIFE OF A MILLENNIAL, THEY'RE DESIGNED TO BE SHARED.

IN THIS SECTION, YOU'LL LEARN:

- HOW TO TURN ANY HOUR INTO HAPPY HOUR
- HOW TO FRY THINGS WITHOUT CAUSING SKIN DAMAGE
- AND OF COURSE, HOW TO LOVE THE FOOD YOU COOK

WHO KNOWS? MAYBE YOU'LL EVEN LEARN TO LOVE YOURSELF A LITTLE MORE, TOO.

PROBABLY NOT, THOUGH.

PROBABLY JUST THE STUFF ABOUT FOOD.

POPOVERS

YOU'D IDEALLY HAVE A POPOVER PAN TO MAKE
THESE, WHICH YOU CAN BUY FOR LIKE $12, BUT
CUPCAKE PANS WILL SUFFICE IF THAT'S ALL YOU
HAVE. IF YOU HAVE NEITHER, WELL, IDK.

FIGURE YOUR SHIT OUT.

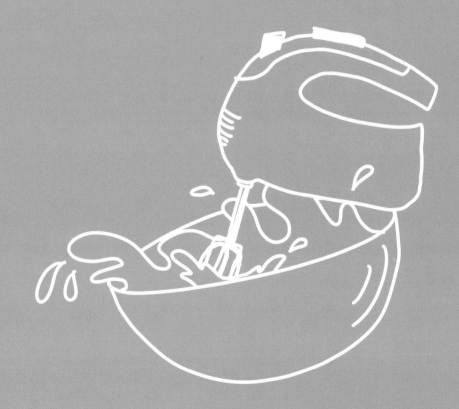

WHAT YOU NEED:

1 ½ tablespoons melted unsalted butter

1 ½ cups flour

1 teaspoon kosher salt

3 extra-large eggs, ideally at room temperature

1 ½ cups milk

Cooking spray

WHAT YOU DO:

1 Using a blender, mix all your ingredients until fully smooth. You can use a whisk too for the forearm workout, if you'd prefer. But that would be dumb.

2 Refrigerate your batter for minimum 2 hours, then remove 30 minutes before you're ready to bake. I don't know why this works, just fucking trust me, okay? Science and shit.

3 Preheat your oven to 425 degrees with your pan inside the oven.

4 When the oven is preheated, remove your pan and generously spray each mold with your cooking spray to ensure the popovers won't stick. Next, pour your batter into each mold until they're about three-quarters full. Bake for 25 to 30 minutes, or until popovers have completely risen and are a beautiful golden brown.

5 Eat them while they're hot. No one likes a cold popover. If you see someone eating a cold popover there's a 99 percent chance they're a serial killer.

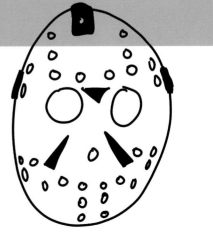

MOZZARELLA STICKS

To be clear, it is perfectly normal to be lactose intolerant but mozzarella stick tolerant.

WHAT YOU NEED:

1 package of string cheese

Canola oil

3 eggs

Panko bread crumbs. They're objectively better than Italian bread crumbs. Not subjectively.

Flour

Marinara sauce (to dip)

The willpower not to make 300 at once

WHAT YOU DO:

1 Freeze your string cheese, then remove from the freezer about 15 minutes before you're ready to cook.

2 Preheat a pan on the higher end of medium-high heat with a thin layer of canola oil coating the bottom.

3 Place 2 small plates and a bowl out on your counter. Line them up so the bowl is between the two plates. In the bowl, crack your eggs. Pour a layer of bread crumbs and flour onto each of the two plates, respectively.

4 Coat each piece of string cheese in the flour first, then the eggs, then in the bread crumbs. This is the exact same process you can follow for frying literally anything.

5 Fry your mozzarella sticks in the oil until all sides have developed a nice, deep, golden-brown texture. Remove from the oil when cooked, then allow them to both cool and drain on a paper towel. Your cholesterol will thank you.

CHICKEN STRIPS

Just like mozzarella sticks, but instead of mozzarella, it's chicken.

NOT MOZZARELLA.
CHICKEN.

WHAT YOU NEED:

I feel like I just said this. Literally the EXACT same thing as mozzarella sticks, but instead of buying string cheese, buy a package of breast tenders from the meat section of your grocery store.

WHAT YOU DO:

1 I feel like I'm talking to a wall here.
Do. The. Exact. Same. Thing. You. Did. With. The. Mozzarella. Sticks. But. This. Time. With. Chicken*.

*The only thing I'll say is make sure you cook these for about 5 minutes on each side, just to make sure the chicken is cooked all the way through. Also, allow them to rest for at least 5 minutes so the chicken can continue to cook after you've fried it.

Sorry for the attitude. Mercury is in retrograde.

CAST-IRON CORN BREAD*

* GET A CAST-IRON PAN. YES, THEY'RE A LITTLE EXTRA WORK, BUT IF YOU CAN TAKE CARE OF YOUR [DOG BREED]DOODLE, YOU CAN TAKE CARE OF A PAN.

WHAT YOU DO:

1 Preheat your oven to 425 degrees, placing the cast-iron pan inside while it preheats, to warm up your pan.

2 Mix the dry ingredients (cornmeal, flour, sugar, salt, and baking powder) together until they're fully incorporated. Do the same with your wet ingredients (milk, buttermilk, eggs), then combine the two until they form one cohesive batter. Did you catch that fancy word I just used? "Cohesive." Pretty cool right? Anyway, add in most of your melted butter to the batter, saving about ⅛ cup for the pan.

3 Once the oven is preheated, remove the pan and turn the heat down to 375 degrees. Add the remaining melted butter to the pan, ensuring the entire bottom is covered, then pour in your mixture. Let that bake for 20 to 25 minutes, then allow 10 minutes to cool.

4 If you want to be super-extra-mega-fancy, you can melt some more butter with about a spoonful of honey mixed in, then pour that over the finished corn bread. Nothing like some homemade honey butter to help you feel better about eating the entire thing.

WHAT YOU NEED:

- 1 ¼ cups coarsely ground cornmeal
- ¾ cup all-purpose flour
- ¼ cup granulated sugar
- 2 teaspoons salt
- 2 teaspoons baking powder
- ⅓ cup whole milk
- 1 cup buttermilk
- 2 eggs, lightly beaten
- ½ cup of salted butter, melted
- Honey, for serving (optional)

cohesive — adj. (I think)
when separate shit
isn't separate anymore

DINNER

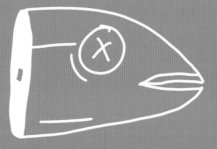

OH, DINNER.

AFTER A LONG DAY OF WORKING AT YOUR OFFICE WITH PING-PONG TABLES AND BEANBAG CHAIRS, DINNER IS YOUR CHANCE TO FINALLY UNWIND. ASIDE FROM THE JUNK FOOD YOU'LL INEVITABLY EAT AT 10 P.M., IT'S YOUR LAST MEAL OF THE DAY. WHILE A GOOD DINNER OFTEN REQUIRES MORE TIME, EFFORT, AND LOVE THAN ANY MEAL, IT'S ALSO WORTH IT.

AND HEY, SINCE A GOOD DINNER TAKES ABOUT AN HOUR, YOU'LL HAVE TIME TO WATCH AN EPISODE OF YOUR FAVORITE TRUE CRIME SHOW.

OR TWO EPISODES OF YOUR FAVORITE WORKPLACE COMEDY.

OR FIVE EPISODES OF YOUR FAVORITE YOUTUBER.

OR 240 TIKTOKS. HAS THE JOKE LANDED YET?

THINK OF DINNER AS A SHINING OPPORTUNITY FOR GROWTH, PRIMARILY IN YOUR STOMACH. YOU ARE THE ARTIST, AND YOUR DINNER PLATE IS THE CANVAS. SO GO. IMAGINE. CREATE. DINNER CAN BE WHATEVER YOU WANT IT TO BE.

EXCEPT SEAFOOD. DINNER CAN NEVER BE SEAFOOD. IF YOU LIKE SEAFOOD, GET THE FUCK OUT OF HERE. WRONG BOOK.

SEASONING **MEAT**

Salt Bae might've actually been on to something . . .

WHAT YOU NEED:

Salt

Pepper

Chili powder

Garlic powder

Onion powder

Lemon, lime, orange

WHAT YOU DO:

I'm not going to write steps here, partially because each meat is different, but also because this is so fucking basic, it doesn't need steps.

In general, if you take a pinch of salt, pepper, chili powder, garlic powder, and onion powder, and you shake that shit up, you've got the perfect seasoning on (or in) your hands. That's it.

For chicken, you can add a fresh squeeze of lemon when you're done.

For pork, the same, but with an orange slice.

For beef, the same, but with lime.

I don't make the rules. I don't know why each meat requires its own respective citrus. It just does. I'm the one who wrote the book, not you. Don't question it.

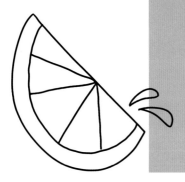

FLANK STEAK

It takes about 5 minutes to cook one of these, which is still twice the amount of time the majority of guys on Bumble last in bed.

WHAT YOU NEED:

The seasonings we just went over

1 flank steak, ½ pound per person you're feeding

Canola oil. Just a splash.

WHAT YOU DO:

1 Get a pan, ideally cast iron, really fucking hot. Like the high end of medium high. If your pan is smoking a little bit right before you put your steak on, you're doing it right. If you set the smoke alarm off while cooking, don't worry. Firefighters are hot and they might rescue you.

2 Season your steak. Add a tiny amount of canola oil, like a tablespoon or two, into your pan, then add the steak. Allow to cook about 3 minutes on one side, then flip. Cook the other side for 2 to 3 minutes, ensuring you see some nice browning on both sides. Flank steak can cook as fast as 5 minutes, but may need up to 10, depending on the thickness of your steak.

2.5 Cook longer if you want your steak closer to medium, or medium well. This cook time is suggested for medium-rare steak, which is also known as the correct way to eat steak.

3 Rest! Rest. Rest. Rest. Like a thirteen-year-old boy whose parents are gone for the weekend, I can not stress how important it is to rest your meat. Give it 5 minutes, then start eating.

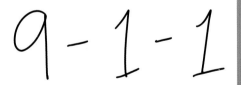

NEW YORK STEAK

BECAUSE NOTHING MAKES A FOOD SOUND MORE APPEALING THAN NAMING IT AFTER A CITY WITH PIZZA RATS.

WHAT YOU NEED:

Seasonings (page 42)
1 New York steak (shocker)
Butter (about ¼ cup)
Garlic. Like a clove or two.

WHAT YOU DO:

1   Get a pan hot (again, cast iron is best). Not *really* fucking hot, like the flank steak. Just hot. Still on the high end of medium-high heat.

2   Season your steak. Put half your butter in your hot pan, then place your steak in and begin to sear. Cook for 6 to 7 minutes on the first side, checking occasionally for color.

3   When your first side has some nice browning happening, flip that shit and do the same thing on the other side. (And *pssssst*, you can flip it more than once. Whoever said you can only flip a steak once and both sides have to be magically perfect is full of shit. Do one hundred flips. Impersonate Simone Biles.)

4   When you flip your steak for the hundredth time, add the rest of your butter and garlic cloves to the pan. Tilt your pan on one side and allow the melted butter to pool with the garlic at the bottom. With a spoon, scoop that melted butter over the steak while it continues to cook. Just writing this is making my mouth water, tbh.

5   Say it with me. Rest. Your. Steak. 5 minutes. Then I guess you can eat or whatever.

"STEAK GYMNASTICS"

BALANCE BEAM

ROAST CHICKEN

You know when people try an exotic meat and then look at you and say, "It tastes just like chicken!" Well so does this. Because it's chicken.

WHAT YOU NEED:

Olive oil (a splash)

Seasonings (page 42)

A whole chicken. Cut up. Ask the butcher you buy it from to do it for you. He (or she) will, and that way, you won't cut a finger off.

1 garlic bulb

Pancetta, aka bougie bacon

WHAT YOU DO:

1 Preheat your oven to 425 degrees, but 420 if you're a stoner. High five.

2 Get a large roasting pan and cover the bottom with a thin (very thin) layer of olive oil. Use a paper towel to make sure the oil covers the whole base of the pan. Season your chicken and place into the pan. Lastly, break the cloves out of your garlic bulb, then peel, cut in half, and sprinkle them over the top of your chicken. Do the same with small pieces of pancetta or bacon.

3 Bake that shit for like 50 minutes. When your chicken has a nice golden brown crust on it, and your garlic and pancetta have both crisped up, that's when you know it's time to pull.

4 Relish in the miracle of poultry that you've just concocted. Those homophobic cows would be so proud.

PESTO PASTA W/ ITALIAN SAUSAGE

Simple. Good. It reminds me of better times, back when . . . well. Actually, idk. History has kind of sucked and humans are the worst. But this pasta? It's good.

WHAT YOU NEED:

Olive oil

Salt

An Italian sausage or two

1 cup of your preferred pasta. I like angel hair, but hey, to each their own. And if you don't know how much a cup is, fuck it. Seize the day. Throw in as much as you want. Pasta is not something to be sparing with.

Pesto. Store bought.

WHAT YOU DO:

1 Fill a pot with water, add a few sprinkles of olive oil and a couple pinches of salt, then bring to a boil. You'll know it's boiling when it's fucking boiling. I'm not explaining that to you. Google it if you have to.

2 Heat a pan over medium-high heat, and when your pan is hot, start cooking your sausage. This will take longer to cook than the pasta, which is perfect, since your pan should heat up before your water boils. To cook your sausage best, slice it in half once it's developed some browning on the outside and cook the now-split sausage face down. Fucking incredible.

3 Once your water is boiling, add in your pasta and cook according to package directions. Then boom. Strain your pasta in the sink. Party's over.

4 In a bowl, add in your pasta with about ¼ cup of your store-bought pesto and mix that up until all your noodles are green. See, healthy, right? It's green. It's basically a vegetable. Add your cooked sausage on top (cut it up if you're smart) and, hey, look at that. You're good to go. You survived another day and ate well.

Google

a how to boil water

Goog Search | feelin' lucky

BURGERS

THE STANDARD. THE HOLY GRAIL OF AMERICAN MEALS. SURE, IT'S JUST A BROWN MEAT DISK, BUT IT'S A BROWN MEAT DISK OF GOODNESS. THERE'S POETRY IN THAT.

WHAT YOU NEED:

Not just any bun, a good bun

⅓ pound of ground beef, turkey, chicken, or bison, I guess?

Seasonings (page 42)

A bit of butter. Just enough to cover the bottom of the pan.

Cheese*

Condiments

* Optional only if you're lactose intolerant or hate joy

WHAT YOU DO:

1 Heat your pan over medium-high heat. Toast your buns, too.

2 Take your ground meat of choice and Van Gogh that shit into a perfect ball. I don't know why I used Van Gogh, I know he's a painter and really this is more of sculpting, but I don't know a famous sculptor, I'm fucking sorry, get off my back. Once you have your perfect ball, smush it down with a spatula until you've got a nice, even, disk shape. Then hit it with some seasonings and you're good to go.

3 When your pan is hot, add your butter and throw that burger on. Bask in the sizzle. But not for more than 4, maybe 5, minutes. Because soon you're going to have to flip it. We can't risk an overdone burger. Medium rare only, as we've discussed. We have standards here.

4 Once it's been 4 minutes, flip your burger. While the other side cooks, go ahead and throw your cheese on now so it can melt.

5 Once the cheese is fully melted, take your burger off and assemble your burger of choice. It's a free** country.

** Technically it's a country catered toward the privileged, primarily based on racial and economic status, but sure, lol, let's go with "free."

VAN GOGH
SCULPTOR?

CAST-IRON PIZZA

So good. Insanely good. Should be illegal how good this is. You'll never want to order delivery again. You will, because it's easy, but let's not ruin a good thing right now.

CAST IRON ZA

WANTED

$1,000,000 REWARD

"JUST TOO FUCKIN GOOD"

WHAT YOU NEED:

Store-bought pizza dough

The cast-iron pan I told you to buy

Olive oil

1 jar store-bought marinara sauce

1 (16-ounce) bag of shred-ded mozzarella cheese

Toppings of your choice, as always. Pro-choice 4ever.

WHAT YOU DO:

1 Take your dough out of the fridge an hour before making your pizza. You want it room temp.

2 Get your oven really hot. As hot as you're comfortable setting it to. If you can go up to 500 degrees, great. I keep mine at 450. The hotter the better though.

3 Give your cast-iron pan a thin coating of olive oil, then form your dough into a nice round pizza, ensuring to cover all the space within your pan. Next, add a layer of sauce (not too heavy) and a layer of cheese (also not too heavy). Less is more when it comes to pizza. Lastly, add your toppings. Or don't. Cheese pizza is cool, I guess.

4 Bake that thing for 15 to 20 minutes, and closer to 25 if you like a really crispy crust. You'll know it's ready to pull when the cheese is starting to brown and bubble on top.

5 Remove and cool for 5 minutes, hahaha just kidding, you're already eating it.

PORK TENDERLOIN

You'll love this recipe so much it will be like family to you. Except they won't ask you to fix their computer because it's "broken" and won't accept their password, even though they just had caps lock on and somehow couldn't see the glowing light.

WHAT YOU NEED:

A pork tenderloin. Size doesn't matter, it's about how you use it.

Seasonings (page 42)

Canola oil

WHAT YOU DO:

1 Preheat your oven to 400 degrees, and start heating up an oven-safe pan on medium-high heat.

2 Season your pork tenderloin. This is what we've been training for.

3 Pour a splash of canola oil in your hot pan, then begin to sear your pork tenderloin. No more than 2 minutes per side. You're not looking to cook it fully. Just to add a little color.

4 Once all the sides of your pork tenderloin are nice and brown, go ahead and stick the pan directly into the oven for roughly 20 minutes, or about 5 minutes per ½ pound.

5 Rest for 5 minutes, as we've discussed in great detail.

6 Take a bite and then fall into a deep depression, knowing you'll never be capable of loving another human quite as much as you love this meat.

dear wife,
i'm leaving you.
for pork tender-
loin. thx bye.

love,
me

LASAGNA

ALRIGHT. THIS ONE IS A DOOZY. MAYBE I'M ASKING TOO MUCH HERE, BUT TRUST ME, IF YOU PULL THIS OFF? IT WILL BE THE STUFF OF LEGENDS. GENERATIONS WILL TELL YOUR STORY. YOU'LL BE IMMORTALIZED IN HISTORY FOREVER.

AND BEST OF ALL, YOU'LL HAVE LEFTOVERS FOR LIKE A FUCKING WEEK.

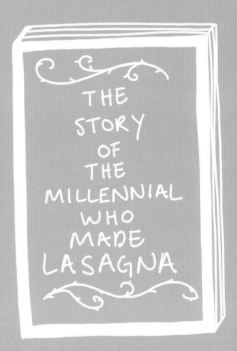

THE STORY OF THE MILLENNIAL WHO MADE LASAGNA

WHAT YOU NEED:

1 ½ pounds ground Italian sausage, mild or hot

A jar of marinara sauce

1 (16-ounce) tub of ricotta cheese, low-fat if you want to be healthy. lol.

1 egg

Garlic salt and pepper

A box of lasagna noodles

Olive oil

1 (32-ounce) bag of shredded mozzarella cheese

MAMA MIA!

WHAT YOU DO:

1 Preheat your oven to 375 degrees, begin boiling a pot of water, and preheat a pan over medium-high heat. Try not to get overwhelmed.

2 Start cooking your ground Italian sausage. You're just looking to get the sausage like 80 to 90 percent done. It will continue to cook in the oven. Once you finish that, turn down the heat to simmer, then pour your full jar of marinara sauce straight into the pan.

3 In a bowl, combine your ricotta with your egg. Add in some garlic salt and pepper for taste, too. Then set that aside.

4 Once your water is boiling, throw in roughly 14 noodles. Also! Very important! Add salt and a splash of olive oil into your water while your pasta cooks. It will keep it from sticking. Cook the noodles for about 6 minutes, then strain 'em and drain 'em.

5 In a large roasting pan, begin to build your lasagna. Spray the pan, then lay down enough noodles to evenly cover the bottom. 3 to 4 at the most. Next, add a layer of mozzarella. After that, add half of your meat sauce. Then, half of your ricotta and egg mixture. Once that's all done, lay down another layer of noodles and do that same thing again. Mozz. Sauce. Ricotta. Finish with one last layer of noodles on top, which should then be generously garnished with what's left of your mozzarella.

6 Bake for 35 to 40 minutes, and broil on low for the final 2 to 3 minutes if you like the top really crispy. Allow to cool for at least 15 minutes, then eat. Eat like you've never eaten before.

DESSERT

HEARTBURN meds

14 TABLETS

FINALLY.

LET'S BE HONEST FOR A SECOND.

BREAKFAST IS SPECTACULAR. LUNCH HAS ITS MOMENTS.
DINNER IS ALWAYS A GOOD TIME.

BUT DESSERT?

WHEN YOU CAN EAT CHOCOLATE CAKE WITH CHOCOLATE
FROSTING IN A POOL OF CHOCOLATE SAUCE WITH A SIDE OF
CHOCOLATE ICE CREAM? NOW THAT'S FUCKING LIVING.

IN THIS SECTION, WE'LL PUSH THE LIMITS OF WHAT SOME
MAY CALL "NECESSARY" HUMAN CONSUMPTION. YOU'LL
LEARN RECIPES THAT WILL MAKE YOUR FRIENDS LOVE
YOU, AND YOUR ENEMIES HATE YOU. IF YOUR ENEMIES ARE
DENTISTS. AND OF COURSE, WE'LL EXPLORE THE DIFFERENCE
BETWEEN A "SUGAR COMA" AND AN ACTUAL COMA.

BUT MOST IMPORTANTLY, I'M DONE WRITING AFTER I FINISH
THIS SECTION.

SO LET'S FUCKING GET ON WITH IT.

CHOCOLATE CHIP COOKIES

A CLASSIC. LIKE THE BEACH AT SUNSET, OR DECADES OF INSTITUTIONAL RACISM AND MISOGYNY.

WHAT YOU NEED:

3 cups all-purpose flour

1 teaspoon sea salt

1 teaspoon baking soda

1 cup white sugar

1 cup light brown sugar

1 cup unsalted butter, softened

2 large eggs

2 teaspoons pure
   vanilla extract

2 cups dark chocolate chips. I'll
   call your mom and tell on you
   if you use milk chocolate and
   she's gonna be, like, so mad.

WHAT YOU DO:

1 Preheat your oven to 350 degrees.

2 In a bowl, combine your flour, salt, and baking soda until they're evenly mixed.

3 In a separate bowl, combine your white sugar, brown sugar, and butter until they too are evenly mixed. Add in your eggs and vanilla, then mix one last time. By the way, try a drinking game where you have to take a shot every time I say "evenly mixed" or "fully incorporated." Have fun.

4 Pour your butter/sugar/deliciousness mixture into the bowl with your flour, salt, and baking soda. Give that a good, even mix, take a shot, then lastly add your chocolate chips into the dough.

5 Refrigerate the dough for at least one hour. It will make the cookies better, I promise—this isn't just science lying to you.

6 Scoop out small balls of your dough and place about 1 inch apart to bake on a lightly buttered cookie sheet for 12 to 15 minutes. The end.

DEEP-FRIED SANDWICH COOKIES

For legal reasons, I can't say the brand of sandwich cookies we all know that I'm talking about. Also, for legal reasons, residents of Arizona aren't allowed to let their donkeys sleep in bathtubs. Seriously. Real law. Look it up.

WHAT YOU NEED:

Canola oil
Pancake mix
Sandwich cookies
Heartburn medication

WHAT YOU DO:

1 Preheat a pot, with enough oil to fill about 1 to 2 inches of the pot itself, over medium-high heat.

2 Make a small bowl of pancake mix. Follow the instructions on the box, I can't do everything for you.

3 Once the oil has warmed up, dip each cookie in the pancake mix, making sure that it's completely coated in batter.

4 Fry your batter-covered cookies in the oil for about 2 minutes on each side, or until they're puffy and brown.

5 Burn your mouth trying to eat them too fast.